A Hope of Wisdom

A Hope of Wisdom

THREE ESSAYS ON EDUCATION

BY

Joseph Addison Clark 1873

James M. Moudy 1973

Victor J. Boschini Jr. 2023

TCU Press

Fort Worth, Texas

Library of Congress Control Number: 2023006472

TCU Press

TCU Box 298300
Fort Worth, Texas 76129

www.tcupress.com

This is number ______

of______ copies, here signed by

Foreword

The word "education" is no commonplace word when Joseph Addison Clark and James M. Moudy use it. It weighs more (it has meaning), it glows more (it inspires) in the texts of those two men.

"Education," one of the words that tends to amble, sometimes to stumble, steps up the pace to a smart trot when those two men put it in the shafts. What is prone to be pedestrian takes off to be a part of the race. It invites you to look at it and speculate.

Joseph Addison Clark was the father of Addison and Randolph Clark, the brothers whose long vision and dedication brought Texas Christian University about. A hundred years later James M. Moudy is chancellor of TCU in 1973. Obviously, the original hope of wisdom is still alive; the same dedication moves TCU.

In perception, conviction, and grace, Joseph Addison Clark, Randolph Clark, Addison Clark, and James M. Moudy are spiritual brothers. Theirs is the same vision of what should be done, the same intention to do it, the same special enabling and ennobling power that is shared by all men and women taught by them.

The first book in the Centennial Series of the TCU Press, 1973, is owing to the generous permission of Dr. R. Lee Clark, president of the University of Texas System Cancer Center in Houston and great-grandson of Joseph Addison Clark.

James Newcomer
Director, TCU Press

January 1973

You never enjoy the world aright . . . till you are clothed with the heavens, and crowned with the stars: and perceive yourself to be the sole heir of the whole world, and more than so, because men are in it who are every one sole heirs as well as you . . . .

Till your spirit filleth the whole world, and the stars are your jewels; till you are as familiar with the ways of God in all Ages as with your walk and table: till you are intimately acquainted with that shady nothing of which the world was made: till you love men so as to desire their happiness, with a thirst equal to the zeal of your own: till you delight in God for being good to all: you never enjoy the world. Till you . . . are more present in the hemisphere, considering the glories and the beauties there, than in your own house: till you remember how lately you were made, and how wonderful it was when you came into it . . . .

Thomas Traherne, 1636? – 1674

Foreword II

"An investment in knowledge pays the best interest."

BEN FRANKLIN

"The function of education is to teach one to think intensively and think critically. Intelligence plus character— that is the goal of true education."

MARTIN LUTHER KING JR.

Fifty years ago TCU Press Director James Newcomer published *A Hope of Wisdom: Two Essays on Education* as part of TCU's centennial celebrations.

In his "Foreword," Newcomer introduced the two essays, one written by Joseph Addison Clark in 1873 and the second written by Chancellor James M. Moudy a hundred years later, in 1973. A century of vast and constant changes separated the two men and their essays. Joseph Addison Clark wrote his essay as his sons, Addison and Randolph Clark, were establishing the AddRan Male and Female College in Thorp Spring, while Chancellor Moudy wrote his essay in Fort Worth as TCU was celebrating one hundred years of progress. Despite the considerable differences of time, location, and context, Newcomer discovered several similarities between the two essays and between the Clarks and Moudy:

In perception, conviction, and grace, Joseph Addison Clark, Randolph Clark, Addison Clark, and James M. Moudy are spiritual brothers. Theirs is the same vision of what should be done, the same intention to do it, the same special enabling and ennobling power that is shared by all men and women taught by them. (iv)

What unites these educators was their devotion to the institution they served and their belief that ultimately education was essential for the well-being of society and the advancement of individuals. Knowledge was power that enabled and ennobled.

Celebrating TCU's sesquicentennial, this current edition of *A Hope of Wisdom* adds a third essay on education, written by Chancellor Victor J. Boschini Jr. Like Joseph Addison Clark and James M. Moudy before him, Chancellor Boschini reflects not only the same devotion to our institution but also the same conviction that education enables and ennobles. The Clark brothers established their college to educate responsible citizens. Learning meant little without shaping character. One hundred years later, Chancellor

Moudy believed that TCU was and should always remain a "values-affirming institution," that facts and information meant little without dignity and integrity. Another fifty years have passed, and Chancellor Boschini has helped steer TCU through economic downturns, difficult issues, and an unprecedented pandemic by strengthening the university's commitment to its mission, vision, and values. While connecting the Clarks and Chancellor Moudy, Newcomer commented that "the original hope of wisdom is still alive, the same dedication moves TCU." With boundless dedication, spirit, and energy, Chancellor Boschini has equally kept this hope of wisdom alive. In commemorating TCU's 150 years, it is appropriate to place his observations next to those of Joseph Addison Clark and James M. Moudy.

Dan Williams
Director, TCU Press

April 2023

1

Education

CONSIDERED IN REFERENCE TO THE INDIVIDUAL

Joseph Addison Clark

Education

CONSIDERED IN REFERENCE TO THE INDIVIDUAL

It is proposed to consider the proper method of education, not as a school system, nor as a plan of instruction best to be pursued in institutions of learning; but the method or plan to be pursued as to the education of the individual, including both instruction and self-education.

Education in all its bearings upon human character and welfare is a subject of the most eminent and vital importance; paramount to all others in the concerns of men; great beyond comparison in the height and depth and scope of its results in the experience of life; because upon this fixed foundation is raised by Destiny the building of Fortune; the fabric of usefulness, or the abode of mischief; the bright mansion of happiness, or the dark prison house of misery. Every person has some sort of education, taking the word in its largest sense; some kind of tree of knowledge growing in the midst of the garden of the mind, whether good or evil, that casts its proper fruit upon the banks of that stream, which, flowing from the same garden, runs around the whole world of that person's affairs. Hence the great desideratum is to adopt the best mode of study and of instruction; the most effectual cause to excite, develop, enlarge, strengthen, discipline, and direct all the powers of the mind; i.e., the intellectual faculties, the moral principles, and the mere affections or propensities; the wisest course to enable the mind to store itself with useful knowledge, and to execute with finished workmanship its own productions, and evolve at pleasure its own originalities; that education that makes the most perfect man.

To act upon a perfect system is the primary rule of education that rides over the top of the whole subject and runs through all of the rules that can be laid down thereon. This rule of action is everywhere illustrated in the universe. When we consider the heavens, the work of God's fingers, we are filled with inexpressible admiration at the beautiful and wonderful system upon which all things are constructed by the Supreme Architect of the universe. When we look at the earth with all its variety of things appearing at first sight as a confused chaos, without form and void, we are upon a closer view again excited, with no less delight and adoration at the admirable harmony that here also prevails, the infinitely skillful adaptation of every means to the end and the wise relation of all the parts to each other and to the whole. "Order is heaven's first law." System is the Alpha and Omega of both divine and human conduct. In all agricultural, mechanical, and mercantile affairs systematic action is the fundamental rule, without which there is no assurance to success. Either in war or peace, in the field or in the council, in the closet of the sage or upon the stage of active life, seldom has it been that anything worthy to be recorded or noticed, anything great or excellent, or durable in its nature, has been achieved without a regular system of action being regarded as the constitutional law of life.

But if system is necessary for others, eminently so is it with the student; if it is necessary in the active scenes of the world, it cannot indeed be dispensed with when preparing for the duties there to be performed. Even the highest order of genius, that seems so peculiar in its origin and character, and often so wonderfully grand and godlike in its works, never, when true to its own nature, acts at random. Light, in all its beautiful variety and composition of colors, and in all its brilliant manifestations and admirable uses, has its fixed laws; that apparently wayward, erratic, and lawless thing, the electrical fire of heaven, in all its startling and awful forms of sublimity, has its unchangeable laws; that strange and mysterious visitant to our lowly world, the intangible spirit of the northern lights, which, with such amazing celerity, "cuts its fantastic tricks" upon the broad arch of the sky, as though the celestial curtain were lifted, and all the angels had come out to dance a pantomime upon the platform of heaven for the amusement of man, that too has its invariable laws of motion from which it does not depart; nor is the solitary comet, that, unlike all the other heavenly orbs, seems to come and go as it listeth, as a lawless wanderer among the solar systems of space, an anomaly in this respect—it has its destined path, its immutable system of laws; nor is it otherwise with the storms and the tempests, the winds and torrents, of the earth. So it is with genius. Although, in its loftiest flights, it may discard the rules prescribed by feebler minds, yet it always, in such cases, acts upon rules of its own creation; "it is a law unto itself." Indeed this is a distinctive mark of true genius—that brightest earthly image of the Godhead—that it works upon a system of its own, makes its own laws.

System, harmony, is the strength and beauty of all things, but more especially of the education of this mind of ours.

God, in the formation of the mind, has pointed with unerring wisdom to this great fact. The mind is wonderfully made; there is a glorious harmony in its construction; and it is the business of education only to trace out the principles and follow the landmarks established by the hand of divine Wisdom. It is its business to erect the temple of learning, with due proportion and elegance and symmetry; to finish, with skillful workmanship and in order, all its walls, and passages, and apartments, and columns, and pillars; and to adorn the whole with the beautiful polish of truth. It is its business to fit up the human mind into a glorious mansion of which its Creator need not be ashamed. System is the fundamental law of education.

The first inquiry, that naturally arises, is—When should education begin? And the answer as naturally and as truly occurs, that it should begin when the infant first begins to learn. Not that the infant should be hurried to school and daily drilled and dragged through a tedious routine of arduous exercises; and the young mind crushed in the premature attempt to load it with artificial knowledge; but there is a large field of parental instruction that should be cultivated before the child ever becomes acquainted with the schoolhouse, and if this were duly attended to, the schoolteacher would have a very different task to begin with from what he generally does. When children, for several years and during that formative period of life, receive their daily lessons in the street and the groggery, and derive their common language from the vocabulary of the abandoned drunkard, the debased libertine, and the profane swearer; or become imbued with the talebearing, backbiting, calumnious, and malicious spirit of slander and vituperation, that too often pervades the family circle; what interesting and promising subjects for an education are they when first they enter the schoolhouse! What hopeful pledges of future excellence when first they appear before the instructor!

There is a widespread and lamentable deficiency in the department of early parental instruction. We seldom consider the great proportions of the whole knowledge of life that is acquired in the years of infancy insomuch that mental philosophers have, for thousands of years, been puzzled in devising theories to explain the fact. Some idea of this may be obtained when we reflect that it is then that not only a language is acquired, but that the *use of language itself* is learned; and this comes to the mind not as a mere set of arbitrary signs, not empty and barren, but pregnant with knowledge; for at the same time that the child learns the name of a tree, he first learns what a tree is; and so of everything else. All the faculties of the young mind are then fresh, and buoyant and active, and continually reaching forward to something new; there is nothing to distract it; no cares to weigh it down; no dark cloud of guilt between it and the light. But we select with the most anxious care the right kind of food for the body; and is there no discrimination to be exercised as to the aliment of the mind? We fence in, and cultivate, and water, and

weed, and loosen the earth around the plants and flowers of the garden; and is there no mental culture required for the virgin soil of the human being?
Must it be left, at the most critical period, like the field that catches all its seeds from the winds and the birds of passage—the field where the worms and the reptiles crawl, and the wild beasts live unscared? But what can be done with so delicate and wayward and intangible a thing as the infant mind? I answer, that as soon as it begins to be disobedient, it can be corrected and brought into subjection. The person who, when a child, is well governed will, when a

man, govern himself. Again, when the infant curiosity first awakens and makes its inquiries, it should never be coldly repulsed as impertinent, as is too often the case; thereby crushing the eager spirit of knowledge; but that curiosity should always be gratified, and encouraged and led forward, and fresh objects pointed out to its pursuit. Thus new and exciting scenes will constantly open up to its delighted view. The intellectual faculties, in the first stage of their growth and strength, should be disciplined; the moral sentiments pointed, by precept and example, to their legitimate objects; the propensities controlled; the evil passions restrained and subdued; and the amiable affections fostered.

When, so well as in infancy and early youth, can many of the mental faculties be practically taught their proper office and limited to their legitimate functions? The spirit of self-defense and the desire to destroy all agencies of evil, from manifesting themselves in forms of quarrelsomeness and cruelty; the inclination to acquire and appropriate things to one's own use, and the disposition to conceal one's own feelings and thoughts and actions from others, from misery into dishonesty and hypocrisy and falsehood; a proper self-respect and a due regard for the approbation of others, from degenerating into haughty pride, overweening egotism, supercilious self-conceit, and omnivorous vanity; a careful cautiousness, from verging into an unmanly fear and cowardice; benevolence into prodigality; firmness into stubbornness and prejudice; veneration into superstition; and hope into idle and empty dreams of the future? When so well as at this auspicious season, can conscience assume its throne; and a sense of justice, a desire to do right in all things, be impressed upon the soul?

The first years of life are the time when moral emotions are the purest, and truest to the nature, of the mental faculties by which they are manifested, and the objects that excite them. The young mind will always form some opinion upon every subject that comes under its cognizance, and act upon that opinion. Here may be inferred the folly, instead of the wisdom, of leaving the child without religious instruction until he comes to years of maturity; when, as is often said, he can judge for himself. He *will* judge for himself much sooner than that; and if the truth is not presented to him he will embrace error. We should certainly teach those under our charge what we sincerely believe to be the truth; and when they come to maturity, they will find it much easier to review the evidences and prosecute their inquiries than they would to grow up, their mind a moral wilderness, and then begin to subdue their prejudices and errors. One generation would derive but little benefit from the past experience of the world, if it must arrive to manhood before it is entrusted with opinions. Samuel, when an infant, was set apart to a religious education; and Timothy knew the holy scriptures from a child.

I suppose, beyond a doubt, that every person, as well as every nation, has by nature a mental constitution peculiar to himself; education makes not all the difference in men; nevertheless, it is apprehended that the character of the man is in a very great degree formed and molded by the education of his childhood; the great outline is then fixed; like the earth, the primitive formations, the continents, the mountains, the oceans, the great rivers, are made permanent; in after years lava may be poured forth, islands cast up, new streams opened, alluvion formed, the surface cultivated and improved, and universal wealth developed, but the impressions of infantile education are hardly less established and durable than the original constitution itself of the mind.

As a second rule upon education: the young student should be taught, at the earliest practicable period, to be always engaged in some *useful* employment; not always toiling, for the mind needs relaxation as well as the body, but then even its amusements may be wisely considered with regard to improvement; the plays of childhood, like the manly sports of the ancient Greeks, may be well adapted with this view; nor by useful is it meant to be overplodding in works of indispensable necessity; but whatever ministers to the welfare and happiness of man, and exalts his character and adorns his mind, is useful. The beautiful and the sublime in poetry; the creations of the chisel and the pencil, produced by the master spirits of genius, although less necessary in this coarse world than some other things, and so worthless and vain in the estimation of some; and yet far from useless, when we consider that the enjoyment of them arises from the exercise of the proper functions of mental faculties bestowed by a wise Creator.

Life at the longest, is but short; time is precious, there is a vast deal to learn; therefore, as a matter of economy, early habits of industry should be cultivated. It is all-essential that a proper sense of the value of time and knowledge, and of the efficiency of continued and rigorous labor should be impressed upon the youthful mind. Therefore early habits of industry, as the medium of converging this truth practically to the mind, should be cultivated. That the mind should always have the complete command of itself and be able, on all occasions, with facility, to turn all its faculties to the best account and avail itself of all its knowledge, is of eminent importance; therefore as a preparation for successful and skillful action in future life, early habits of industry should be acquired.

A third inquiry upon this subject: What proportion of time should be employed in study? No definite rule, applicable alike to all cases, can be laid down upon this point. From the diversity of general physical constitution, cerebral organization, and mental temperament; from the various degrees of the power of concentrativeness in different minds, as well as the infinite variety of combination of the mental faculties in different persons; what would be only intellectual pastime to one would be intolerably burdensome to another; but taken in connection with the foregoing remarks upon the necessity of early industrial habits, a great degree of improvement requires that sleep, study, and recreation should each have a regular and fixed portion of every day allotted to them; and in times of mental relaxation let the body be exercised in some manly employment; nor let useful labor be despised; the mind will return with renewed vigor to its pursuits. Here, the great utility of manual labor schools may be observed. Were these generally adopted, how many thousands of students might be saved from imbecile idleness and consequent degrading vice and crime! And again, how many thousands more might be saved from worthlessly sacrificing themselves victims to incessant study without a corresponding exercise of body and physical and mental repose! If we were all intellect, ceaseless and sleepless thought might, perhaps, do; if we were mere animals, inactive sloth might be consistent with our nature; but as, in this life, we are neither mere spirit nor mere matter, but a compound of both so far as we can judge from our mental manifestation, both the mind and the body being mentally dependent upon and affected by each other; it is well to avoid those extremes in the habits of the student—the Scylla and Charybdis of education; namely, incessant study and mindless idleness; to avoid the evil of each by the joint exercise of both mind and body in useful labor; for there is a real dignity in labor, and it should always constitute a part of education.

A fourth inquiry presents itself, namely: What is the best manner of studying? For the same reasons stated under the last head of this essay, no precise general rule can here be laid down. Inasmuch as the mental character of no two persons appears to be the same, no formula can be given by which every mind can contemplate any subject. Hence the narrow-minded folly of any one that undertakes to require others to study exactly according to his particular mode—to lie upon his Procrustean bed; to see through his eyes; and learn and think with his mental organs. But some useful suggestions may be made upon this topic. First, every study should be thoroughly understood before another one is taken up. Superficial study is a general evil with the scholar. Some studies, when once tolerably acquired, need not be dwelt upon; for the subsequent use of the facts and principles involved in them will render them familiar; thus it is not necessary to linger upon the alphabet, for its use in every subsequent stage of the spelling book fixes it indelibly in the memory of the learner;

so with the four fundamental rules of the arithmetic, they enter into the solution of all subsequent questions. In every department of life, when first principles are sufficiently acquired, practice is then the most effectual lesson; and the scholar, at every stage of education, should learn to use the knowledge previously acquired. But the evil, wished to be particularly noticed here, is the habit of hastening ignorantly from one study to another. It is better to understand a few branches of education well, than to have a smattering knowledge of many; it is much better to read a few books well, than to devour or skim over numberless volumes. Many students have passed through the regular routine of study in a careless manner and graduated at college; and then have found it necessary to begin and educate themselves. Many others, without undertaking this severe task, have passed on through life, with a merely nominally liberal education.

Secondly, the undivided attention should be given to any subject while studying it. For this purpose but one thing should be undertaken at a time; the mind should be wholly withdrawn from the contemplation of all other things; and the student should retire, as much as possible, into solitude and, for the time being, bury himself in his particular pursuit; all distracting things should be avoided. Hence may be inferred the egregious folly of those schools, if schools they can be called, when all study or rather gabble aloud—like bedlam! It is necessary to know how to think and act in scenes of excitement, in the noise and the crowd, among men, but common sense teaches us that these are not fit places for the student to go with his book. It is true, that in order to acquire a correct education, other things besides books should be studied. Men and actual things are the original materials of thought. Education consists in a correct knowledge of objects that exist, of events, and of the properties and relations of things; and wherever these are presented to the mind, as some of them everywhere may be, there is the original subject for study.

Thirdly, there should not be a mere passive attention on the mind, but, by a determined and vigorous effort of the will, there must be an active and continuous application to the subject to be learned. The human mind is not like a block of marble that can be chiseled by the sculptor; nor a machine that can be moved at the pleasure of another. Unlike every thing in the universal world, it can be improved only in and through its own volitions. It must labor for itself, it must educate itself. We often hear of self-educated men; and this, in the common acceptation of the terms, is all well enough; but, after all, although one may have more of the appliances of instruction, and the facilities of education, and have fewer obstacles to overcome than another, yet strictly speaking, there is no other than self-education. We read comparatively too many mere facts, and reflect too little. We are instructed comparatively too much, and study too little. Here may be remarked the futility of expecting to get a competent knowledge of any science by merely listening to lectures thereon. Here, too, may be noticed the fact, that in the religious world, there is by far too little general study in proportion to the amount of preaching. Self-application is the keystone to mental progress. There are labor-doing machines, but there never will be an educating machine. The road to learning may be macadamized and improved by many inventions, but the student will, nevertheless, always have to travel on foot.

A fifth and very important matter is—the proper order of pursuing different studies; that is, what branches should be attended first? The knowing faculties, i.e. such as take cognizance of individual things that exist, and of events and the properties of things, namely: size, form, color, etc., are in active operation much sooner than the higher order of intellectual powers, including the reflective faculties, come to any degree of maturity. Hence the attention should be first turned to those branches in which the exercise of the former only is to any great degree necessary; namely: reading, writing, geography, and history. Grammar and arithmetic cannot be extensively studied to so good an advantage at an early age. A common mistake is the dabbling with other languages before having learned one's own. One may be a good English scholar without knowing any other language; if he cannot be a philologist, he certainly can be a good grammarian; and however much the dead languages, as well as some that are now spoken, may be useful in enabling one to acquire a complete and philosophical knowledge of the English, as well as of the principles of language generally, yet it is certainly the dictate of wisdom and of common sense that he should learn how to use his own mother tongue respectably before he enters upon the path of the linguist. Let this scholar first learn the principles of universal grammar in his own language, and then he will be prepared to understand the particular rules of another language. The rudiments of a common education should first be completely mastered before the higher branches are meddled with. A reasonable attention to this rule would save a great deal of the awkwardness and embarrassment that are met with in the world.

A sixth and last but not the least inquiry is: What to study? The answer to this question has, in a considerable degree, already been anticipated. It should be a settled point with everyone to acquire the rudiments of a common English education, if possible; and this can be done, in a moderate degree, at least, by nearly all if they will. I go further, and say that it is the duty of everyone who has the means, to give himself what is commonly called a liberal education. All that is learned there will be useful, whatever calling or profession he may afterwards pursue. But this question admits of a definite answer in two respects. In the first place, after having finished the ordinary academical or college education, what particular business or profession should the individual pursue? Let anyone consider, from the history of his own mind, let him observe to which does his own inclination instinctively turn; and these inquiries will resolve themselves into a rule which, if followed, he will be very likely to go right. An attention to this rule would have saved many an individual the chagrin and misery of having embarked in a wrong profession, when he might have been much more useful and happy in some other calling. In the second place—what course of reading and study should be followed after entering upon one's profession or particular pursuit? Of course his principal attention should be given to that which relates directly to his own profession; and more especially to his actual business. If he is familiar with the textbooks, he will be prepared to apply the principles to particular cases. But he that confines himself to the books of his own profession will come far short of excelling even in that profession. Every truth has some relation to every other truth; and general knowledge upon all branches elevates and enriches the mind and enables it to take a larger view of things. Literature, science, and especially the true philosophy of man are essential to the highest degree of excellence in any profession. Many have professed to despise literary pursuits and studies, especially that class of them often denounced as fictitious writings; but those men that have been most distinguished in their profession have not refused to notice them, and improve and adorn their minds with these productions of genius. That there have been many novels written which are not worth reading, there is no doubt; and the same is equally true of books upon every other subject. That many persons occupy too great a portion of their time in reading those novels that are good in themselves, is equally true; and the same is true of good books upon other subjects. There seem to be many persons who can take no pleasure nor derive any benefit from such productions; so there are those that see nothing but mortar and stone and wood in the noblest works of architecture; nothing but a rock in the most skillful workmanship of the sculptor; nothing but daubed canvass in the works of Raphael's genius.

There are those that can look without an emotion of beauty, or grandeur, or sublimity, upon the works of nature; but should we therefore shut our eyes upon these things? Because some seem to have no idea of anything but mere facts and absurd principles, because they seem to have no faculty (to much extent) for appreciating the beautiful and the sublime, and do not appear to understand what we mean by the ideal. Must we therefore mortify these high faculties which God has given us, and regard the exercise of them a sin? Let us not be wise above the Creator. Let us attend to His hand writing in the organization of the human mind, to the things that are prepared for its contemplation in the works of Nature and of human genius.

I cannot close this essay without saying that the Bible should be the great book of study at every stage of education and of life. His education is most miserably deficient who is not acquainted with its truths and its beauties.

2

Toward Wonder

EDUCATION AND RECOGNITION

James M. Moudy

Toward Wonder

EDUCATION AND RECOGNITION

Boy-child, girl-child, man, woman —all of us are wonders. And we live amid wonders.

Yet too easily and too much we accustom ourselves to the wonder of the world and of each other. Too seldom and too shallowly we probe even what we *can* fathom of it all. Most only blink at existence, then pass away. Others peer more intently, try to say what joy or sorrow they can make of it, and then too pass away. None, however, sees everything. Nor can any say half of what he sees.

No matter. Even if any saw it all and could say it all, it's better that he not set it all down, for then we would be wonder-less, and we would come to the end of both mystery and mankind.

The essay of Joseph Addison Clark, which precedes this one, engages to say something that bears on both wonder and mystery: he writes of "education." His essay and mine must be read as attempts to deal with mixtures of irrefutable observations and unprovable inferences, for what we call "education" is not an exact science and probably cannot become so: principles that seem certain at one time are at other times uncertain (or perhaps it is only people that are uncertain). Uncertainty, however, is no necessary obstacle to belief. And so Clark put down his beliefs about education, as so shall I, and the reader may have his own opinion as to their certainty.

Not all are agreed as to the original meaning of the word "education." That it is from the Latin *educere* meaning "to lead out" or "to lead forth" (cf. "educe" and "ductile") is likely. But is emphasis to be focused on a drawing forth of what is *already there*, or is the proper emphasis a *molding*, *forming*, *shaping* of what is drawn out? If to "draw forth," the process of education has only the goal of getting it out. If to "mold," the process is to stamp and form the emerging, waiting, malleable person-to-be.

That we don't know what the word "education" really means is, fortunately, not disabling. We do not need a solution before proceeding. Man easily adapts to living amid what he doesn't understand. And good thing, else he would petrify. The bad part is that he takes for granted too much and thereby misses most of the wonder.

So, while we don't really understand education, we educate. We give education considerable attention, really. We bow down to it for reasons good and bad.

Besides, for some it is a living. And for too many it is also a dying.

We regard education as such a good thing that we want to perpetuate it, so we institutionalize it. This makes education die as much as live, for to institutionalize idea or process is to humanize and so to restrict it. Anything that is humanized comes at least partially under the rules of the human condition, including aspiration and despair, success and failure, best and worst, otherness and selfishness—and living and dying.

The systems and processes of institutionalized education have in this year of our Lord 1973 reached heights and depths never before attained. Could anyone have predicted, did anyone predict, that, even before mankind could really afford it, large numbers would leave off grubbing for bodily sustenance and give themselves to filling the mind; and that, after the introduction of labor-multiplying machines, such vast numbers of persons for so large a part of their lives would be enabled, perhaps even compelled, to devote themselves to the giving and receiving of education?

The largest, most expensive, and most diverse systems of education are found in the United States. Here, too, must also be found the best and the worst of such systems: the best and the worst would *have* to be found amid the largest. (Though impossible in the space of this essay, a story in itself would be to suggest to what extent our educational systems are unplanned and alternativeless substitutes for society's inability to introduce our burgeoned population into, and occupy it successfully in, a machine-production economy that needs consumer-people more than the people really need the production machines.)

Of more importance than schools and systems of education are (1) *learning* and (2) *teaching*. Let us put aside the institutional aspects and consider these.

Strictly speaking, education means teaching, not learning, for one can learn without being taught. Indeed, perhaps most of what is learned is not achieved via teaching. Learning comes earlier and looms larger than teaching. So learning might take a logical precedence in this discussion.

How learning takes place and is achieved is observable but not greatly understood. In learning, something physiological happens, but what? And is it only physiological? There must be more than that. But we still don't know for sure.

For now, the only clue that learning has taken place is a *change* in the learner.

Here is a key both to learning and to changing people. Whatever a person learns, by that much he is changed. He will never again be as he was, for learning is never accomplished without a change being worked in the learner.

(The converse is not entirely true, however. It appears that one can change by two other means: insight and will. There is no way to account for insight and will through the ordinary or natural learning process. Insight and will must, therefore, be beyond natural processes, must be *super*natural. Or so I believe.)

Learning is inevitably followed by change. Nor is there any way for a person to make any progress whatsoever (other than mere bodily growth) except that he learn and change. All human development, aside from the merely physical, therefore, depends upon learning. And the learning begins at least at the moment of birth (some say prenatally).

Perhaps it should here be remarked that, though learning always causes change, what one learns does not necessarily result in change in *behavior*. Though the mind inexorably is altered following learning, nothing guarantees that behavior will be altered. Outward behavior is never a true, complete, undistorted reflection of what is in the mind.

Habit and will enter here (and *won't* does, too). Thus, for example, few parents act out more than a modest portion of what they know about child development and child rearing, and few teachers perform as well as they know how.

Learning takes place only in encounters with the *unfamiliar* (a person cannot learn what he already knows). Thus he can develop only as he encounters newness. It should not then surprise us that opportunities for learning are directly proportional to the availability of encounters with newness. What this means for parents and other teachers has been worth volumes and merits others.

It is also clear that no one can learn for another. *But one can help another learn*, and here enters the role of the teacher. Here, also, enters education, for, not until teaching occurs is there, strictly speaking, education. Although education sometimes takes place unintentionally when someone causes another to learn without meaning to, in its pure form *education is a conscious effort on the part of one or more to stimulate, facilitate, hasten, and multiply learning in a person or persons.* (The teacher also learns as he teaches and in doing so he becomes a learner; but this reciprocal action is not a necessary consideration, for education is essentially a onedirectioned process.)

Parents and other family members are, of course, the earliest teachers. But their preoccupations and varying abilities and preferences have—from earliest recorded time to the present—caused them to depend upon a corps of "teachers" to carry on the main tasks of human development. While there are elements of abdication in this shift, there are also wisdom and intention in it, for by and large the results are more successful than if only family members had been the teachers.

Advantage is also found in carrying on this intentional promotion of learning at places or centers outside the home. Such centers multiply opportunities for new encounters, the basic preconditions of learning. Sadly, this possibility is thwarted all too often by schools that are actually less active in offering learning encounters than are some of the homes and families.

Timing is also crucial in learning. Recently there has been a growing recognition that teachers and schools enter the child's life much too late, especially for the child from a home marked by uncaring or deprivation. Why have we waited until age six to send the child to school? It has been generally assumed that age six was the earliest the child could be secure and competent in finding his way to and from the schoolhouse across the local landscape. Such considerations are hardly now pertinent. The tradition of beginning first grade at age six must be broken quickly, for irretrievable months and years of high learning-readiness have been lost by that time.

If children ordinarily start school too late, it may also be true that they stay in school too long. Are they not now so physically and psychologically advanced at age seventeen and eighteen that they are ready for something quite different from being high school juniors and seniors? Do not so many uninterrupted years of school, school, school violate the students' needs and endurance? If the answers are "yes," and I think they are, it would make economic and humane sense to try a system that starts two to four years earlier and ends one to three years earlier.

However, systems at best are only facilitative. They should not get in the way. It is not to our credit, or to our children's betterment, that we deal so much in systems. It is better to talk of the people who educate.

Foremost among the people important to education are parents. None has greater opportunity and therefore greater responsibility than they. When we consider the likelihood that for unrecorded millenia they and other members of family or tribe were the only teachers, it is clear that their educative role was crucial and not unperformed. That they should be the main teachers is the natural form of education. Today the worst error of our modern approach to education is that parents and family have been so much excluded from the role of educators for children.

However, even should parents uniformly serve their teaching role at a high level, it is clear from the rate of progress since teaching specialists have been widely used that teachers have been extremely useful to society; and it would be hard to say they are not now indispensable. Theirs is a great calling (some in and some out of the profession have missed their calling), and they deserve higher honor and reward than they have yet received.

What is a good teacher? Perhaps the clue is found more in what he is than what he knows. The signs are clear that success in the calling of a teacher is only secondarily related to his subject-matter preparation. Of primary importance is the teacher as a person. His perceptions and initiatives in stimulating learning are more crucial to his role of promoting learning than is his store of facts. The student can do a surprising amount of learning on his own if only well stimulated, especially at college age; and because of this fact, colleges and universities are especially blameworthy for their hyper-attention to subject-matter credentials of prospective faculty and for their inattention to teaching effectiveness.

Fortunately, as already implied, the learner does not *have* to wait on his teacher. Indeed, if none ever went beyond his teacher, never could there be progress. That most generations do exceed their predecessors is proof that the role of the learner is more crucial than that of teacher. We will do all a favor if, at least by the time the learners in our school have reached early teens, we strongly impress on them that the major responsibility in education is theirs, not their teachers'.

Let me conclude with some remarks concerning curriculum. "Curriculum" means in its etymology "a race or course to be run." So defined, the word has a forbidding aspect, drawing more attention to the route than to the goal. Our constant tinkering with curriculum is evidence of our preoccupation with means instead of ends. That curriculum is subject to the imbalance of faddists at times and to the inertia of embattled subject-matter devotees at other times evinces our philosophical groundlessness as well.

Fortunately, the paths and stopovers of the curricular race course are of less than surpassing importance. Whether curriculum changes or not is of remarkably little effect as compared with the results of good teaching. The better the teachers, the less important the curriculum. Indeed, good teachers *are* the best curriculum.

But, to the extent that curriculum *is* important (and if anyone *feels* it is important, then his views must be dealt with), it must be built on learners' needs, not on teachers' interests. So the fundamental question underlying curriculum is, “What do the learners need to know?” More pertinently, what do young learners in a latter-twentieth century USA need to know? A favorite answer to this question employs the term “liberal arts.” Originally the “liberal arts” consisted of grammar, rhetoric, and logic (the “trivium”) and arithmetic, music, geometry, astronomy (the “quadrivium”). Does this list correspond to what is taught today in the so-called liberal arts college? It does not, of course. There is considerable ground for suspicion that many who praise the liberal arts have little concept of the historic meaning of the phrase.

But “liberal arts” does offer a useful

understanding via the root meaning of "liberal," coming from *liber*, meaning "free," or, better, the "free person." *The liberal arts are those things a free person needs to know, things that free the mind*—and only in the mind can full freedom be approximated.

Briefly, as I see them, studies that can free the mind are, in their order of importance:

(1) knowledge of God,
(2) of one's world,
(3) of self,
(4) of others, and
(5) of communicating with others.

This order is not, to be sure, the order

in which the mind first meets these subjects. Restated in the sequence one encounters them developmentally, they are: knowledge of one's world, of others, of self, of communicating, and of God. The infant's first mental awareness is of the "outside," the world. Next, soon—surprisingly soon, at that—he distinguishes other human beings as a class and as *his* own caretakers in particular. Just how and when he also comes to awareness of self, and whether this awareness precedes or follows his recognition of communications to him by others, and his to them, cannot really be ascertained. Last in the sequence, apparently, is a knowledge of

God, which knowledge he first obtains from others (though to some a knowledge of God is given directly, or it is somehow created within, for at least once in history such had to occur, else none would have any concept of God).

All subjects ever devised by curriculum makers fall under the above-named topics. Unfortunately (or so I believe) not all curricula include all these topics, and mankind is the poorer on this account.

Recent curricula in the United States are relatively most attentive to teaching about the world and about others, somewhat attentive to the arts of communication, relatively less attentive to teaching about self, and relatively least attentive to teaching about God. That is a summary of how I see it, and perhaps I should elaborate.

Recent attention to science, engineering, and technology probably has caused these subjects to be the strongest portions of our curricula. Despite this strength, however, the principles of science are not taught comprehensively, most schools settling for brief laboratory experiences in one or two sciences. While this deficiency is serious, it is not nearly so serious as other curricular deficiencies.

A greater deficiency is in our teaching about others. In the United States we have depended too much on narrow slices of our own history, have introduced few students to sociology and social psychology, and have introduced even fewer to the way a national economy works. How much the average citizen needs to understand these social studies, as compared with scientific and technological studies, can be seen in the answer to the question, "How often is the citizen asked to vote on matters scientific, as compared with how often he must vote on matters of societal importance?" While the need for a large supply of highly trained scientists and engineers is clearly evident to a technological civilization, that need is pretty well met. But the need for a citizenry well educated in economics and politics is very poorly met.

As for the arts of communication, including what is rudimentarily called reading and writing, here is something everybody talks about but fewer and fewer accomplish. The problem can be traced to a very simple source, namely, the decreasing attention being given to the *practice* of writing and speaking. The communication arts, like all art, are only mastered by long practice. It would appear that the more there is to read and study and the more there is to communicate about (and the more to communicate to), the less time we have (or take) for the necessary practice. The decline in penmanship, as compared to only one or two generations earlier in the United States, seems marked by a similar decline in knowing how to put words together. And is there not a necessary connection, since both involve the inescapable necessity of practice?

Current curricula weaknesses in natural sciences, social sciences, and communication arts, bad as they are, are probably exceeded by the scant attention to teaching individuals about themselves, and surely exceeded by the relative decline in recent decades of teaching about God. Without study of psychology and religion, how can one deal with the dicta, "Know thyself" and "The fear of the Lord is the beginning of wisdom"?

Of these two subjects, psychology is still a very young topic and not yet widely respected, and so it is not hard to understand why it is not prominent in our common studies. It deserves respect, and it must be more practically and more widely incorporated into our curricula.

But theology is the oldest study of all, and it is hard to understand why most moderns have backed away from it. The modern's frequent denial—real or pretended—that he should have either beliefs or knowledge about theology and religion is probably a sign of his embarrassment at his ignorance of both. Most PhDs haven't an equivalent primary-school level of knowledge about the subject; and because they are the nation's curriculum-makers, these doctors of philosophy ("teachers of the love of knowledge"), and doctors of education as well, do their greatest disservice by showing their partiality for (and insecurity outside of) their own specialties. Their inability (or is it disdain? or only ignorance?) to see the whole need of students and their preoccupation with the safer world of their own specialties are both the sources of limited successes in teaching and harbingers of decreasing effectiveness.

Yet—and I regard this judgment as categorical—despite the vast importance of both parental and professional teaching efforts and despite the disarray of most curricula, the responsibility of the individual learner is supreme. Mankind's greatest gift is its potential, and though the potential of each is finite (probably), the mind, once it is led through the early doorways of learning, is for all practical purposes unfettered, free to roam at will, to reason, to compare, to deduce, to intuit, and yes, to value and to believe. No amount of pride, prejudice, ignorance on the part of curriculum-planners, neglect or weakness on the part of parents and teachers, and no pressure of job or diversion via affluence, can be cited as a necessary obstacle to the autonomous learner. For him, education was only a push, a door-opener, and a challenge. Now, if he will, he can venture beyond what any before him either learned or imagined, into the veritable unknown of that which "eye hath not seen, nor ear heard, nor entered into the heart of man, what God hath prepared for them that love Him."

Such is the ability of man the learner. Through education the parent and teacher attempt to provide him larger openings to the wonder that he is and to the wonders amid which he lives. Viewed educationally, one is torn between a despair at how blind and unknowing most of us remain and an elation at the triumphs of at least a few spirits who entered into the record their knowings and imaginings. That they did this even before they went on to discover whether their truths were True, and before they came to know even as they are Known, is to their everlasting credit, and is worthy of our emulation.

3

What is a TCU Education?

Victor J. Boschini Jr.

What is a TCU Education?

I thoroughly enjoyed reading and re-reading the essays by Joseph Addison Clark, father of Addison and Randolph Clark, and Dr. James M. Moudy, who served as chancellor from 1965 to 1979. Mr. Clark wrote his essay in 1873, as his sons were starting the AddRan Male and Female College, while Dr. Moudy wrote his essay in 1973, as Texas Christian University was celebrating its first one hundred years. Framed by the times in which they lived, their perspectives are still worthy of consideration. Both of these men left their own special mark by pondering the question ***what is a TCU education***? They both remarked on the wonders of education by offering their own observations and inferences. And now, as TCU celebrates its 150th anniversary, it is my honor as chancellor to share my views.

First, permit me to provide some context and how my views have been shaped by what I have experienced. My career in higher education has spanned more than forty years and has included administrative teaching positions at seven different universities, ranging in size from 2,000 to 40,000 students. From my vantage point, TCU is an exceptional place that fosters collaboration for the greater good. We do this by establishing a setting where everyone has a place at the table and deserves to be heard, where we remain committed to educating ethical leaders and responsible citizens. I believe that TCU has a unique connection culture that not only supports but also nurtures students. This culture contributes to the success of our graduates, who leave TCU confident and equipped with a global mindset and with high values and goals to make a difference in their communities—and beyond.

Personally, I think the best aspect of a Texas Christian University education is that both the professor and the student converge in a campus setting as learners. TCU has a rich and remarkable history of providing a living laboratory where an individual can experiment and learn by missteps or failure with a safety net, or learn by accomplishment with the coaching and encouragement of others. This is what an education is all about. Students grow under the guidance and care of an incredible cadre of faculty and staff.

Stepping out with courage and curiosity, TCU students possess an adventurous spirit that allows them to push their limits, expand their horizons, and, ultimately, develop new perspectives. This great desire for growth through exploration still exists today on the TCU campus, as it did one hundred and fifty years ago. To get the full picture of a TCU education, visit various areas on campus where learning and mentoring take place. Look at the student poster presentations in the College of Science & Engineering that reveal brilliance and aptitude. In the Harris College, witness nurses in training show compassion and model reflective listening to better understand the needs of clients and patients. In Fine Arts, attend a student theatre production of professional quality, an art show to see student artists showcase their exceptional artistic talent, or a student dance performance in Erma Lowe Hall, where passion is captured in creative movement. In Neeley, listen to students pitch their venture ideas and leverage their business skills with innovation to solve problems and make a social impact on communities. Equally powerful and inspiring learning can be found in AddRan, Education, Communication, Honors, and our newest school, the Anne Burnett Marion School of Medicine, one of the most innovative medical programs in the country. Suffice to say, our students dare to be different and share their knowledge, talents, and abilities because of the support and encouragement they receive on campus. The Clarks opened their school in 1873 as a student-centered campus, and so TCU remains today.

The hallmark of a TCU education has always been the value-added bonus that comes from caring and dedicated professors and staff members. A well-rounded approach to learning has been there since the beginning and will continue beyond our 150 years of existence because of the dedicated people we attract to teach, serve, and support our students. As a caring campus community, TCU offers an abundance of learning experiences both curricular and cocurricular.

One of my favorite things to do as Chancellor is visit with students over lunch or dinner. I find that breaking bread together allows us to move past the formalities and form relationships. I often ask students for feedback on what they like the most about TCU and what could be done to make TCU even better. Students are candid and share some amazing insights with me. I delight in encouraging a student with an idea and watching that idea come to fruition in one form or another. This is what fulfills and motivates me as an educator, and this is what is best about a TCU education.

Recently, with the passing of Chancellor Emeritus Dr. William E. Tucker, I had the opportunity to reread his speeches and reflect on his inspirational words. He was a wonderful mentor and friend to me, and I always looked forward to our interactions. I miss him and wonder how he would have responded to the question ***what is a TCU education***? I found clues to Dr. Tucker's response in these remarks he gave at TCU's Convocation in 1989:

I expect every student here to recognize and honor the only basic reason for the existence of this University. Contrary to the well-intentioned but short-sighted pronouncements of many experts, a student's purpose is not to accumulate semester hours, not to complete a major. A student's purpose is not to make a 3.5 grade point average, not even to earn a degree. The student's overarching purpose is to become an educated person.

Dr. Tucker carried forth this mantra as he mentored thousands of students, faculty, and staff. He noted, "An educated person moves through every stage of life's adventure in gratitude for the privilege of learning, growing, serving." He further noted his expectations that every TCU student "be a contributing member of the community seeking to become educated." We honor Bill Tucker's legacy, and the legacy of other TCU leaders who have gone before us, by perpetuating expectations to "be a contributing member of the community seeking to become educated."

On this glorious occasion of TCU's sesquicentennial, may we each embody an "attitude of gratitude," and continue to be grateful for opportunities in this lifetime to learn, to grow, and to serve as educated people of high values and goals. May we continue to promote a caring campus culture that connects us and encourages us to live up to our greatest potential.